# Finding *Joy* in the Journey

MAX LUCADO

WORD PUBLISHING
Dallas · London · Vancouver · Melbourne

**Finding Joy in the Journey**

Published by Word Publishing



ISBN 08499-5213-1

Printed in the United States of America

## *Finding Joy in the Journey*

*THEY'RE ALL around us—little nuggets of joy, pebbles on the roadside. Small moments of blessing—just waiting to be gathered up. Pocket-size joys, like an unexpected smile or a kind gesture. a quiet morning with an old friend. Sometimes we're blinded by the harsh winds of crisis.*

*We all face frustration, boredom, pain. But joy is a choice. Either we choose to dwell on the negatives or we stop and look for the joy.*

*There is joy in the journey. And most remarkable of all, we are loved by the Father. What greater joy could there be!*

*Chapter One*

# Glory in the Ordinary

THERE IS one word that describes the night he came—*ordinary*.

The sky was ordinary. An occasional gust stirred the leaves and chilled the air. The stars were diamonds sparkling on black velvet. Fleets of clouds floated in front of the moon.

It was a beautiful night—a night worth peeking out your bedroom window to admire—but not really an unusual one. No reason to expect a surprise. Nothing to keep a person awake. An ordinary night with an ordinary sky.

The sheep were ordinary. Some fat. Some scrawny. Some with barrel bellies. Some with twig legs. Common animals. No fleece made of gold. No history makers. No blue-ribbon winners. They were simply sheep—lumpy, sleeping silhouettes on a hillside.

And the shepherds. Peasants they were. Probably wearing all the clothes they owned. Smelling like sheep and looking just as woolly. They were conscientious, willing to spend the night with their flocks. But you won't find their staffs in a museum nor their writings in a library. No one asked their opinion on social justice or the application of the Torah. They were nameless and simple.

An ordinary night with ordinary sheep and ordinary shepherds. And were it not for a God who loves to hook an "extra" on the front of the ordinary, the night would have gone unnoticed. The sheep would have been forgotten, and the shepherds would have slept the night away.

But God dances amidst the common. And that night he did a waltz.

The black sky exploded with brightness. Trees that had been shadows jumped into clarity. Sheep that had been silent became a chorus of curiosity. One minute the shepherd was dead asleep, the next he was rubbing his eyes and staring into the face of an alien.

The night was ordinary no more.

The angel came in the night because that is when lights are best seen and that is when they are most needed. God comes into the common for the same reason.

His most powerful tools are the simplest.

❧

Consider the rod of Moses.[1] By this time in his life, Moses had been a shepherd as long as he had been a prince, and he'd grown accustomed to it. Herding sheep wasn't as lively as living with Egyptian royalty, but it had its moments, especially the moment God spoke to him through a burning bush that didn't burn up. God announced that Moses was his man to deliver the Israelites. Moses wasn't convinced he was the one for the job. God said that who

Moses was didn't matter; what mattered was who God was. And God set out to demonstrate.

"Moses," spoke the voice from the bush, "throw down your staff."

Moses, who had walked this mountain for forty years, was not comfortable with the command.

"God, you know a lot about a lot of things, but you may not know that out here, well, you just don't go around throwing down your staff. You never know when . . ."

"Throw it down, Moses."

Moses threw it down. The rod became a snake, and Moses began to run.

"Moses!"

The old shepherd stopped.

"Pick up the snake."

Moses peered over his shoulder, first at the snake and then the bush, and then he gave the most courageous response he could muster.

"What?"

"Pick up the snake . . . by the tail." (God had to be smiling at this point.)

"God, I don't mean to object. I mean, you know a lot of things, but out here in the desert, well, you don't pick up snakes too often, and you *never* pick up snakes by the tail."

"Moses!"

"Yessir."

Just as Moses' hand touched the squirmy scales of the snake, it hardened. And Moses lifted up the rod. The same rod he would lift up in Pharaoh's court. The same rod he would lift up to divide the water and guide two million people through a desert. The rod that would remind Moses that if God can make a stick become a snake, then become a stick again—

then perhaps he can do something with stubborn hearts and a stiff-necked people.

Perhaps he can do something with the common.

❧

Or consider another shepherd from Bethlehem.[2]

There are certain things anyone knows not to do. You don't try to lasso a tornado. You don't fight a lion with a toothpick. You don't sneeze into the wind. You don't go bear hunting with a cork gun. And you don't send a shepherd boy to battle a giant.

You don't, that is, unless you are out of options. Saul was. And it is when we are out of options that we are most ready for God's surprises.

Was Saul ever surprised!

The king tried to give David some equipment. "What do you want, boy? Shield? Sword? Grenades? Rifles? A helicopter? We'll make a Rambo out of you."

David had something else in mind. Five smooth stones and an ordinary leather sling.

The soldiers gasped. Saul sighed. Goliath jeered.

David swung. And God made his point. "Anyone who underestimates what God can do with the ordinary has rocks in his head."

❧

Or what about the blind man Jesus and the disciples discovered?[3]

The followers thought he was a great theological case study.

"Why do you think he's blind?" one asked.

"He must have sinned."

"No, it's his folks' fault."

"Jesus, what do you think? Why is he blind?"

"He's blind to show what God can do."

The apostles knew what was coming; they had seen this look in Jesus' eyes before. They knew what he was going to do, but they didn't know how he was going to do it. "Lightning? Thunder? A shout? A clap of the hands?" They all watched.

Jesus began to work his mouth a little. The onlookers stared. "What is he doing?" He moved his jaw as if he were chewing on something.

Some of the people began to get restless. Jesus just chewed. His jaw rotated around until he had what he wanted. Spit. Ordinary saliva.

If no one said it, somebody had to be thinking it: "Yuk!"

Jesus spat on the ground, stuck his finger into the puddle, and stirred. Soon it was a mud pie, and he smeared some of the mud across the blind man's eyes.

The same One who'd turned a stick into a scepter and a pebble into a missile now turned saliva and mud into a balm for the blind.

Once again, the mundane became majestic. Once again the dull became divine, the humdrum holy. Once again God's power was seen not through the ability of the instrument, but through its availability.

"Blessed are the meek," Jesus explained. Blessed are the available. Blessed are the conduits, the tunnels, the tools. Deliriously joyful are the ones who believe that if God has used sticks, rocks, and spit to do his will, then he can use us.

We would do well to learn a lesson from the rod, the rock, and the saliva. They didn't complain. They didn't question God's wisdom. They didn't suggest an alternative plan. Perhaps the reason the Father has used so many inanimate objects for his mission is that they don't tell him how to do his job!

It's like the story of the barber who became an artist. When asked why he changed professions, he replied, "A canvas doesn't tell me how to make it beautiful."

Neither do the meek.

That's why the announcement went first to the shepherds. They didn't ask God if he was sure he knew what he was doing. Had the angel gone to the theologians, they would have first consulted their commentaries. Had he gone to the elite, they would have looked around to see if anyone was watching. Had he gone to the successful, they would have first looked at their calendars.

So he went to the shepherds. Men who didn't have a reputation to protect or an ax to grind or a ladder to climb. Men who didn't know enough to tell God that angels don't sing to sheep and that messiahs aren't found wrapped in rags and sleeping in a feed trough.

❧

A small cathedral outside Bethlehem marks the supposed birthplace of Jesus. Behind a high altar in the church is a cave, a little cavern lit by silver lamps.

You can enter the main edifice and admire the ancient church. You can also enter the quiet cave where a star embedded in the floor recognizes the birth of the King. There is one stipulation, however. You have to stoop. The door is so low you can't go in standing up.

The same is true of the Christ. You can see the world standing tall, but to witness the Savior, you have to get on your knees.

So . . .

while the theologians were sleeping
and the elite were dreaming
and the successful were snoring,
the meek were kneeling.

They were kneeling before the One only the meek will see. They were kneeling in front of Jesus.

*Chapter Two*

# Joy in the Journey

SHE SAT in 14E, and I sat in 14D. She was rural, and I was urban. She was backward, and I was sophisticated. She was homey, and I was "professional." But she could see, and I was blind.

"They sure do put these seats close up against each other, don't they," she said as I sat down.

Her face was ten inches from mine. She had basset-hound cheeks; her eyebrows peaked over her nose; and her jowls sagged. She smiled so widely you could see the cavity on her upper side. Her neck seemed to lean out of her shoulders at a forty-five-degree angle, leaving her head in front of her shoulders rather than above them. She wore a Dutch-bob haircut and a blue, velour pants suit.

I don't know if she was old or just looked old. But I do know one thing: She'd never flown.

"I don't do this too much, do you?"

When I told her I did, her eyes widened. "Oooh, that must be fu-un." (She could add a syllable to any word.)

I groaned to myself. I already had a bad attitude. My week had been hectic. The plane was late and overbooked. I had a toothache and had left the tooth medicine at the hotel. I wanted to sleep, but I had work to do. And now I was sitting next to Gomer Pyle's mother.

"Oooh, boy, look at that one!"

She pointed at the plane ahead of us on the runway.

"Is this one that big?"

"Yes." I hoped my brief response would show her that I wasn't up for chitchat. It didn't.

"I'm going to see my boy in Dallas. Do you ever go to Dallas? I hope he's OK. He had a stomach flu last week. He's got a new dog. I can't wait to see it. It's a Labrador. Do you know what that is? They are big and lovable and . . ."

She was uncanny. Not only could she add a syllable to every word, she could answer her own questions.

As we were taking off, however, she got quiet. For several moments she said nothing. Then she suddenly let out a sound that would have called the pigs for dinner.

"Oooooeeee, those trees down there look like peat moss!"

People seated around us turned and stared like I was E. F. Hutton.

"What river is that?"

I told her I didn't know, so she flagged down a stewardess.

When the drinks came around, I asked for a Coke; she asked for the list.

"Tell me again?" So the stewardess told her again. "Oh, it's so hard to choose," she giggled. But she finally chose.

When they brought her the drink, she exclaimed that she didn't know apple juice came in cans. And when they brought her a sandwich, she opened the box and proclaimed loud enough for the pilot to hear, "Why, they even put mayonnaise in here."

When I pulled out my laptop computer, she was enthralled. "Now isn't that clever."

And that went on . . . the whole flight. She didn't miss a thing. If she wasn't staring out the window, she was amazed by a magazine. If she wasn't talking, she was "oooh-ing." She played with her fan. She turned her light on and off. She toyed with her seat belt. She savored her lunch. When we went through turbulence, I looked over at her to be sure she was all right, and she was grinning. You'd have thought she was riding the Ferris wheel at the county fair!

It occurred to me, about mid-journey, that she was the only person enjoying the trip.

The rest of us, the "sophisticated," were too mature to have fun. The man in front of me was discussing business trips to Japan, dropping more names than the U.S. Bureau of the Census. The fellow behind me was ordering beers—two at a time. The lady to my right was up to her eyebrows in paperwork. And I was staring at a computer screen—eyes tired, mouth hurting, stressed-out, trying to find a message for stress-filled people and never noticing that the message was sitting beside me.

And I might never have noticed had she not leaned over and said to me at the end of the flight. "Son, I may be out of place in saying this, but you've worked the entire trip. You need to relax, boy. You need to put that machine up and enjoy the journey."

Gulp.

I smiled weakly and mumbled some excuse about needing to get the work done before tomorrow. But she wasn't listening. She was squeezing her hands together in excitement as we landed.

"Wasn't that a fu-un trip?" she asked as we were leaving the plane.

I didn't say anything. I just nodded and smiled. Off she walked, bouncing down the concourse as curious as a six-year-old. I watched her as long as I could, then turned to go to my next flight with a lesson learned.

I resolved to keep my eyes open.

It does little good, I decided, to make the trip and miss the journey.

*Chapter Three*

# Remarkable

SOMETHING HAPPENED a few weeks ago that could be filed in the folder labeled "Remarkable."

I was playing basketball at the church one Saturday morning. (A good number of guys show up each week to play.) Some are flat-bellies—guys in their twenties who can touch their toes when they stretch and touch the rim when they jump. The rest of us are fat-bellies—guys who are within eyesight of, if not over the top of, the hill. Touching our toes is no longer an option. Looking down and *seeing* our toes is the current challenge. We never touch the rim when we jump and seldom touch it when we shoot.

But the flat-bellies don't mind if the fat-bellies play. (They don't have a choice. We have the keys to the building.)

Anyway, a few Saturdays back we were in the middle of a game when I went up for a rebound. I must have been pretty slow because, just as I was going up for the ball, someone else was already coming down with it. And the only thing I got from the jump was a finger in the eye.

When I opened my eye, everything was blurry. I knew my contact lens was not where it used to be. I thought I felt it in the corner of my eye, so I waved out of the game and ran to the rest room. But after I looked in the mirror, I realized that it must have fallen out on the floor somewhere.

I ran back onto the court. The guys were at the opposite end, leaving the goal under which I had lost my contact lens vacant.

I hurried out, got down on my knees, and began to search. No luck. When the fellows started bringing the ball downcourt, they saw what I was doing and came to help. All ten of us were down on our knees, panting like puppies and sweating like Pony Express horses.

But no one could find the silly lens.

We were just about to give up when one fellow exclaimed, "There it is." I looked up. He was pointing at a player's shoulder. The same guy whose finger had explored my cornea.

There, on his shoulder, was my lens. It had fallen on him . . . stuck to his skin . . . stayed on his back all the way down the court while he jumped and bounced . . . and then ridden all the way back.

Remarkable.

Even more remarkable when you consider that the contact lens made this round trip on the back of a flat-belly. One of the guys who can touch the rim and his toes. Had it landed on the shoulder of one of the "top-of-the-hill guys," no one would have been impressed. Some of us have the mobility of grazing buffalo. But when you think of the ride the tiny piece of plastic took, when you think of the odds of it being found, you have only one place to put this event: in the folder labeled "Remarkable."

The more I thought about this event, the more remarkable it became.

The more remarkable it became, the more I learned about remarkable things.

I learned that remarkable things usually occur in unremarkable situations, i.e., Saturday morning basketball games.

I also noticed that there are more remarkable things going on than those I usually see. In fact, as I began to look around, I found more and more things that I'd labeled "To be expected" that deserve to be labeled "Well what do you know."

Examples?

My money is in a bank with at least several thousand other folks' money. Who knows how many transactions are made every day? Who knows how much money goes into that place and is taken out? But somehow, if I want some money or just want to know how much money I have, the bank teller can give me what I want.

Remarkable.

Each morning I climb into a truck that weighs half a ton and take it out on an interstate where I—and a thousand other drivers—turn our vehicles into sixty-mile-per-hour missiles. Although I've had a few scares and mishaps, I still whistle while I drive at a speed that would have caused my great-grandfather to pass out.

Remarkable.

Every day I have the honor of sitting down with a book that contains the words of the One who created me. Every day I have the opportunity to let him give me a thought or two on how to live.

If I don't do what he says, he doesn't burn the book or cancel my subscription. If I disagree with what he says, lightning doesn't split my swivel chair or an angel doesn't mark my name off the holy list. If I don't understand what he says, he doesn't call me a dummy.

In fact, he calls me "Son," and on a different page explains what I don't understand.

Remarkable.

At the end of the day when I walk through the house, I step into the bedrooms of three little girls. Their covers are usually kicked off, so I cover them up. Their hair usually hides their faces, so I brush it back. And one by one, I bend over and kiss the foreheads of the angels God has loaned me. Then I stand in the doorway and wonder why in the world he would entrust a stumbling, fumbling fellow like me with the task of loving and leading such treasures.

Remarkable.

Then I go and crawl into bed with a woman far wiser than I . . . a woman who deserves a man much better looking than I . . . but a woman who would argue that fact and tell me from the bottom of her heart that I'm the best thing to come down her pike.

After I think about the wife I have, and when I think that I get to be with her for a lifetime, I shake my head and thank the God of grace for grace and think, *Remarkable.*

In the morning, I'll do it all again. I'll drive down the same road. Go to the same office. Call on the same bank. Kiss the same girls. And crawl into bed with the same woman. But I'm learning not to take these everyday miracles for granted.

Just think, it all came out of a basketball game. Ever since I found that contact, I've seen things a lot clearer.

I'm discovering many things: traffic jams eventually clear up, sunsets are for free, Little League is a work of art, and most planes take off and arrive on time. I'm learning that most folks are good folks who are just as timid as I am about starting a conversation.

I'm meeting people who love their country and their God and their church and would die for any of the three.

I'm learning that if I look . . . if I open my eyes and observe . . . there are many reasons to take off my hat, look at the Source of it all, and just say thanks.

*Chapter Four*

# The Sacrificial Visitor

LET ME DESCRIBE A SCENE to you and then ask you to come back to it at the end of the chapter.

An old man walks down a Florida beach. The sun sets like an orange ball on the horizon. The waves slap the sand. The smell of saltwater stings the air. The beach is vacant. No sun to entice the sunbathers. Not enough light for the fishermen. So, aside from a few joggers and strollers, the gentleman is alone.

He carries a bucket in his bony hand. A bucket of shrimp. It's not for him. It's not for the fish. It's for the sea gulls.

He walks to an isolated pier cast in gold by the setting sun. He steps out to the end of the pier. The time has come for the weekly ritual.

He stands and waits.

Soon the sky becomes a mass of dancing dots. The evening silence gives way to the screeching of birds. They fill the sky and then cover the moorings. They are on a pilgrimage to meet the old man.

For a half hour or so, the bushy-browed, shoulder-bent gentleman will stand on the pier, surrounded by the birds of the sea, until his bucket is empty.

But even after the food is gone, his feathered friends still linger. They linger as if they're attracted to more than just food. They perch on his hat. They walk on the pier. And they all share a moment together.

Got the scene? Now put it on the back burner for a few minutes.

❧

*Jesus left there and went along the Sea of Galilee. Then he went up on a mountainside and sat down. Great crowds came to him, bringing the lame, the blind, the crippled, the mute and many others, and laid them at his feet; and he healed them. The people were amazed when they saw the mute speaking, the crippled made well, the lame walking and the blind seeing. And they praised the God of Israel.*

*Jesus called his disciples to him and said, "I have compassion for these people; they have already been with me three days and have nothing to eat. I do not want to send them away hungry, or they may collapse on the way."* [1]

This is not the day that Jesus fed the five thousand men; it is the day he fed the *four* thousand. Although the events have much in common, they are different in several respects:

- When Jesus fed the five thousand, he was with Jews. When he fed the four thousand (plus women and children), he was in Decapolis, a Gentile region.
- When Jesus fed the five thousand, he taught and healed them. When he was

with the four thousand, there is no record that he taught—only that he healed.
- When Jesus was with the five thousand, he was with them for one afternoon. When he was with the four thousand, he was with them for three days.

And for three days he did a most remarkable thing: He healed them. "The lame, the blind, the crippled, the mute and many others" came to him, Matthew wrote, "and he healed them."

Many times I wish that the New Testament writers had been a bit more descriptive. This is one of those times. "And he healed them" is too short a phrase to describe what must have been an astonishing sight.

Let your imagination go. Can you see the scene?

Can you see the blind husband seeing his wife for the first time? His eyes gazing into her tear-filled ones like she was the queen of the morning?

Envision the man who had never walked, now walking! Don't you know that he didn't want to sit down? Don't you know that he ran and jumped and did a dance with the kids?

And what about the mute who could speak? Can you picture him sitting by the fire late into the night and talking? Saying and singing everything and anything that he had ever wanted to say and sing.

And the deaf woman who could now hear. What was it like when she heard her child call her "Mamma" for the first time?

For three days it went on. Person after person. Mat after mat. Crutch after crutch. Smile after smile. No record is given of Jesus preaching or teaching or instructing or challenging. He just healed.

"The people," Matthew wrote, "were amazed when they saw the mute speaking, the crippled made well, the lame walking and the blind seeing." Four thousand amazed people, each telling a story grander than the other. In the midst of them all is Jesus. Not complaining. Not postponing. Not demanding. Just enjoying every minute.

Then Matthew, still the great economizer of words, gave us another phrase on which I wish he would have elaborated:

"They praised the God of Israel."

I wonder how they did that? I feel more certain of what they *didn't* do than of what they did do. I feel confident that they didn't form a praise committee. I feel confident that they didn't make any robes. I feel confident that they didn't sit in rows and stare at the back of each other's heads.

I doubt seriously if they wrote a creed on how they were to praise this God they had never before worshiped. I can't picture them getting into an argument over technicalities. I doubt if they felt it had to be done indoors.

And I know they didn't wait until the Sabbath to do it.

In all probability, they just did it. Each one—in his or her own way, with his or her own heart—just praised Jesus. Perhaps some people came and fell at Jesus' feet. Perhaps some shouted his name. Maybe a few just went up on the hillside, looked into the sky, and smiled.

I can picture a mom and dad standing speechless before the Healer as they hold their newly healed baby.

I can envision a leper staring in awe at the One who took away his terror.

I can imagine throngs of people pushing and shoving. Wanting to get close. Not to request anything or demand anything, but just to say "thank you."

Perhaps some tried to pay Jesus, but what payment would have been sufficient?

Perhaps some tried to return his gift with another, but what could a person give that would express the gratitude?

All the people could do was exactly what Matthew said they did. "They praised the God of Israel."

However they did it, they did it. And Jesus was touched, so touched that he insisted they stay for a meal before they left.

Without using the word *worship,* this passage defines it. Worship is when you're aware that what you've been given is far greater than what you can give. Worship is the awareness that were it not for his touch, you'd still be hobbling and hurting, bitter and broken. Worship is the half-glazed expression on the parched face of a desert pilgrim as he discovers that the oasis is not a mirage.

Worship is the "thank you" that refuses to be silenced.

We have tried to make a science out of worship. We can't do that. We can't do that any more than we can "sell love" or "negotiate peace."

Worship is a voluntary act of gratitude offered by the saved to the Savior, by the healed to the Healer, and by the delivered to the Deliverer. And if you and I can go days without feeling an urge to say "thank you" to the One who saved, healed, and delivered us, then we'd do well to remember what he did.

❧

The old man on the pier couldn't go a week without saying "thank you."

His name was Eddie Rickenbacker. If you were alive in October 1942, you probably remember the day that he was reported missing at sea.

He had been sent on a mission to deliver a message to Gen. Douglas MacArthur. With a handpicked crew in a B-17 known as the "Flying Fortress," he set off across the South Pacific. Somewhere the crew became lost, the fuel ran out, and the plane went down.

All eight crew members escaped into the life rafts. They battled the weather, the water, the sharks, and the sun. But most of all, they battled the hunger. After eight days, their rations were gone. They ran out of options. It would take a miracle for them to survive.

And a miracle occurred.

After an afternoon devotional service, the men said a prayer and tried to rest. As Rickenbacker was dozing with his hat over his eyes, something landed on his head. He would later say that he knew it was a sea gull. He didn't know how he knew; he just knew. That gull meant food . . . if he could catch it. And he did.

The flesh was eaten. The intestines were used as fish bait. And the crew survived.

What was a sea gull doing hundreds of miles away from land?

Only God knows.

But whatever the reason, Rickenbacker was thankful. As a result, every Friday evening this old captain walked to the pier, his bucket full of shrimp and his heart full of thanks.

We'd be wise to do the same. We've much in common with Rickenbacker. We, too, were saved by a Sacrificial Visitor.

We, too, were rescued by One who journeyed far from only God knows where.

And we, like the captain, have every reason to look into the sky . . . and worship.

## CHAPTER ONE
## GLORY IN THE ORDINARY

*"Blessed are the meek, for they will inherit the earth."*

1. How does chapter 1 interpret the word *meek?* How does that definition differ from your previous ideas of "meekness."

2. Do you think of yourself as "ordinary"? Why or why not? Do you find that description comforting or insulting?

3. What are some synonyms for the word *meek* as it is used in the Beatitudes? For ideas, look up Numbers 12:3, Psalm 25:9, Isaiah 11:4, 61:1, Matthew 11:29, and 1 Peter 3:4 in the King James version and another translation.

4. Practically speaking, what does it mean to be meek in the sense of letting God use you? If he doesn't speak through an angel or a burning bush, how do you know what he wants you to do?

5. In practical terms, how do you avoid taking over or "telling God how to do his job"—and still get something done?

6. Psalm 37:11 also states that the meek will inherit the earth. Read Psalm 37:1–17 to understand this verse in context. What is the message of the psalm? Is its thrust basically similar or different from the third

beatitude? What new perspective does Psalm 37 give to Jesus' statement?

7. Describe one time in your life when you let fear keep you from doing something you knew you should do.

## CHAPTER TWO
## JOY IN THE JOURNEY

1. It's easy to judge people, isn't it? Read the following verses: Leviticus 19:15; Proverbs 24:23; Acts 10:34; Romans 10:12; Galatians 2:6.

   When have you made judgments that you shouldn't have made about others and missed what you could have learned from them?

2. When has your journey been interrupted by a lesson you needed to learn? What lesson did you learn? Was it a lesson that you need to be reminded of frequently?

3. How might Jesus' words about an abundant life (John 10:10b) relate to your lifestyle? If you could do three activities this week just for fun, what would they be? In what ways could you add joy to the routine activities in your life?

## CHAPTER THREE
## REMARKABLE

1. After reading this chapter, and its list of "remarkable" things, what remarkable aspects of your life do you tend to overlook? How might your life be different if you recognized more of the remarkable occurrences of everyday life?

2. Read Job 38:4–39:30; 40:9–41:11. How do these images expand your view of the remarkable?

3. Think back to the events surrounding the second most stressful day in Jesus' life (Matthew 14:1–21; Mark 6:7–44; Luke 9:1–17).

   What remarkable things do you think the disciples could easily have overlooked on that day? If they had seen those things as truly remarkable, how might their responses have been different?

   As you observe these events and the disciples' responses, what parallels do you see in your own life?

4. Read 1 Thessalonians 5:18. For what remarkable things can you now give thanks?

## CHAPTER FOUR
## THE SACRIFICIAL VISITOR

1. Matthew 15:29–32 records Jesus' healing of many people and their praise for the "God of Israel." But Jesus didn't preach at them; he just reached out to help them. What does this teach you about what sharing Christ with a hurting world really means?

2. Read Luke's version of this event (Luke 8:1–10). How do Matthew's and Luke's versions differ? In which aspects are they similar? What does Luke's account reveal about the disciples' faith?

3. Read John 3:16; Matthew 1:21; John 10:9; John 1:29; Revelation 5:12; Hebrews 7:26, 27.

In what ways have you been saved by a Sacrificial Visitor—Jesus Christ?

4. A miracle occurred in Rickenbacker's life that kept him alive. What miracle has God done in your life or in the life of someone you know?

   Rickenbacker gives buckets of shrimp to sea gulls to show his gratitude. What can you give to God to say "thank you"?

5. The crowds were amazed when they saw what Jesus had done (Matthew 15:31). How do you respond when God does something special in your life? Write down four things for which you can praise—or worship—God today.

## *Notes*

### Chapter 1—Glory in the Ordinary

1. See Exodus 4:1–4.
2. See 1 Samuel 17.
3. See John 9:1–6

### Chapter 4—The Sacrificial Visitor

1. Matthew 15:29–32.